LEADING PROJECTS

GET YOUR PROJECT OFF THE GROUND

If you don't know why you're doing a project and who's supporting it, you're heading for failure! At the start of any project, you and your team should make sure that the project purpose is clear, you have senior management support, and you know who the stakeholders are.

In this course I'll show you some great tips and techniques. You'll find out how to determine the main project elements, and identify the sponsor and stakeholders. You'll also learn how to collect project requirements, clarify scope, and set key milestones – all the things you need to know in order to get your project off the ground successfully.

Getting Started

1. Defining the Project
2. Identifying Project Stakeholders
3. Determining Project Requirements
4. Clarifying a Project's Scope
5. Setting Milestones
6. Exercise: Getting Your Project off to a Good Start

DEFINING THE PROJECT

Projects are temporary – they usually have a specific start and end date – and they are unique – they're different from other operations. So what makes your project different? What is its unique goal?

To explore those questions, let's say you've been given responsibility to manage a project – getting FDA approval for a new drug. What do you need to know? What are the first steps you take?

Before you start work on your new project, you identify the senior manager who's sponsoring the project. The sponsor authorizes the project, ties it to the greater business goals and objectives, and backs it financially – or may represent the customer's needs. He or she is the link to management, driving enthusiasm within the organization. Get as much information as you can from the sponsor to identify what's needed for success. Ask the right questions to find the answers you need to get off to a good start – for example, "Who are the key people in the organization that I'll be dealing with?" Also, get the sponsor's commitment to see the project through and the authorization to start.

OK now – now that you know who's supporting you, let's take a look at all the other elements that will come into play. They're like the pieces of a puzzle that you'll use to assemble a full picture. As well as the sponsor, there's the purpose of the project, the objectives, any key dates, the resources and budget – which are what allow the project to live and breathe – the key risks, and any assumptions or constraints.

We're going to look at each of these elements in a little more detail, and we'll use the hypothetical drug approval project as our running example.

We already know that you have a sponsor – the next thing you have to do is find out the purpose of the project. The purpose is the reason for initiating the project, and states the business problem that the project will resolve. It must be aligned with organizational goals. In the new drug example, the purpose is fairly obvious – to take the drug successfully through the approval process – but you still might wanna ask questions such as "Will we need to tailor our testing to other countries' approval requirements, or are we seeking approval only in the United States?"

Once the purpose is taken care of, the next objective is to identify the project's objectives. The project team and senior management must agree on the end goal and specific objectives. These should be specific and measurable. From the beginning, a project needs to have obvious success factors to gain buy-in from the stakeholders, to show what was done, and to establish when the request has been satisfied. So in our example, the main objective is clear – get approval for the drug. You might say things like "Do we want advance publicity for the new drug? If so, I'll plan on working with marketing during the approval process."

So far, so good. Now you need to identify the key dates – starting and ending dates, and checkpoints to monitor progress. In the drug approval process there are clearly defined steps that will help you to do this: for example, you could ask "By what date do we need to complete testing?"

Now it's time to identify the resources and budget – resources could be people, material, equipment – whatever is needed to support the project. Your primary concerns here are "What are the resources and budget, and do I have authority and control over them?" For example, in the new drug scenario you might ask "How much can we spend for testing on humans and animals?"

OK – you've come this far. Next, you need to identify the key risks

– all the things that might present a problem or obstacle. Here, you could ask "Are there any other competitors developing a similar drug?"

Now it's time to consider assumptions about the scope, the resources, the funding, the approach we'll use, and other project variables. For example, you might ask "Can we assume that this drug qualifies for the FDA's fast-track program?" Assumptions must be as realistic as possible.

Finally, you identify constraints – initial limitations, such as fixed due dates or budget. For instance, a due date might be set in stone but the budget might have some flexibility. Talk to the sponsor as early as possible to identify these constraints. For example, you might ask "Is there contingency in the budget to fast-track testing if this drug qualifies?"

So, all the initial elements of the project have come together, and you've successfully defined it! You're now ready to begin planning in more detail to reach those project objectives.

IDENTIFYING PROJECT STAKEHOLDERS

You've been appointed to manage an important project – getting FDA approval for a new drug. What will you need to know to do your job properly?

One important step is to find out the people, groups, or organizations that will be involved in the project or may influence it – the stakeholders. These are people like the customer, sponsor, end users, business partners, and regulatory agencies.

Of course it's best if you know who's supportive and who is unsupportive, and especially those that are unsupportive, so that their issues can be resolved early in the project. Identifying a stakeholder late in the project may lead to costly changes.

So, how will you identify those stakeholders? First you can just think about who might be involved. Ask the project sponsor, look at past projects, identify employees who do related work. In your drug approval project, the scientist in charge of research would normally be a stakeholder.

Not surprisingly, some stakeholders are more important than others. Key stakeholders are the ones with the potential to affect the project's progress and outcome. Anyone in a decision-making or management role can also be a key stakeholder. In your drug project, for example, a production manager may be a key stakeholder.

Next, after you've identified the stakeholders, you can classify them. You might think about their level of power, which is the ability to make decisions and facilitate or hinder progress. Also, their influence – their ability to persuade, coerce, or motivate people to bring about change. Interest is the stakeholders' desire to ensure that project outcomes fulfill their requirements. And impact is the degree to which a stakeholder and their actions or inactions could affect the project's success.

Also, you might find it useful to analyze the stakeholder using a matrix. First, decide which two characteristics will help you analyze your stakeholders. Then their position in the grid can guide you in deciding how you'll engage with them. Let's have a look at an influence–interest matrix.

Those with high interest and high influence should be engaged constantly and managed closely: this means getting their input on project events, and often their authorization. The sponsor will fall into this quadrant.

Stakeholders with high influence and low interest you'll need to keep satisfied. They must buy into your project, but they don't want constant communication. Senior management will appear here: you'll contact them on major issues and to report good news.

Those with high interest and low influence should be communicated with frequently but they don't have the authority to make project decisions.

Those with low interest and low influence don't need frequent communication, and you won't need to prioritize their requests. But you might want to monitor them in case things change.

You'll definitely find it useful, as you identify your stakeholders, to create a document that lists them all, along with their contact information and their association with this project. This is called a stakeholder register, and you're going to be referring to it a lot! You can also add to it each time a new stakeholder is identified.

DETERMINING PROJECT REQUIREMENTS

Let's say you've been given responsibility to manage a project – getting FDA approval for a new drug. Before you can plan your work, what will you need to know?

Well, you'll certainly need to know the project's requirements – the criteria by which the stakeholders will judge the result. These are the basis for defining the project's scope, and also for planning and controlling work, costs, time, and quality. Once you know them, you'll have a much better chance of keeping the key stakeholders happy by ensuring the project meets their needs.

On the other hand, if you fail to determine the project requirements, you risk your project falling behind schedule and going over budget. And that certainly is not going to please the stakeholders.

Once you get started, you'll likely find that requirements cover a whole range. There are business requirements – for example, that support growth of the organization by diversifying the product mix. There are functional requirements – a testing program that must achieve certain established standards. There's also performance requirements, safety requirements, compliance requirements, acceptance criteria, assumptions, and constraints. Quite a lot of things to think about!

OK, let's look at some steps you can take to collect those requirements: basically you'll either gather or facilitate requirements, refine and rank those requirements, and then determine how decisions will be made about which ones are in scope, and then finally document those requirements.

In order to achieve this, you can gather information from stakeholders by meeting and sharing ideas. Or, in some cases, you could build a prototype based on a benchmark, and generate requirements from that.

There's quite a number of different tools and techniques that can be used to gather information in several ways.

You can conduct one-on-one interviews with stakeholders and others who can help you identify the features a product or service should have. You'll ask the person a set of questions that you've prepared as well as any other questions that might come up, and then record their responses. For example, if I'm testing a drug on a large number of people, will that improve its chances of gaining approval? Even though it may be very expensive: is it really worth doing?

Facilitated workshops are another great way to gather information by bringing key stakeholders together to define product requirements especially when the stakeholders are from different functional areas of the organization. Because of their interactive group nature, well-facilitated sessions can build trust, foster relationships and improve communication among all the participants.

Focus groups are a less formal way of collecting project requirements. In a group of stakeholders and subject matter experts, you guide an interactive discussion about what a proposed product or service must deliver. This can help you find out the stakeholders' expectations. Usually a focus group includes stakeholders with similar roles or perspectives and will focus on a very specific aspect, such as the product's design or its technical requirements. In your case, of course, the priority is to make sure that the drug fulfills all the FDA's requirements.

Questionnaires and surveys let you gather responses to written questions, and get information from a very large group of people very quickly. The resulting information can usually be evaluated using statistical analysis.

Creative brainstorming or mind mapping - these are useful ways to get groups of stakeholders with different perspectives to generate and share ideas.

In the next step, final decisions will be made about which requirements are in scope. This involves classifying and prioritizing requirements, as well as rejecting some: such as those that have no chance of being able to enhance the approval process. To do this, you can use group decision-making techniques.

For example, decisions can be made by a unanimous agreement among stakeholders, or by a majority, or the greatest block may decide: for example, if 40% are pro, 35% are con, and 25% are undecided, the 40% block will carry the decision. There is also dictatorship, where one person makes the final decision.

[A chart with the heading Group Decision-making Techniques is shown. The first technique described is Unanimity, where 100% of stakeholders must agree on a decision before it is acted upon. The Delphi Technique can be used to achieve anonymous consensus without bias. The second technique is Majority, where more than 50% of stakeholders must support the decision. The third technique is Plurality, where the largest block decides. The final technique is Dictatorship, where one individual makes the decision for the group.]

You'll find it useful to document requirements in a matrix or spreadsheet. What we're looking at here is called a requirements traceability matrix, which is often used for this purpose.

We all make mistakes. So there are some common mistakes that people make in figuring out project requirements. And if you avoid them, it'll make your job a whole lot easier! So, here's what not to do.

Don't leave out key stakeholders who know what's involved in the project. Don't forget to map the requirements to the project's purpose or objective that was stated on the statement of work or to the way they will be tested. Don't accept all requirements: only those that map to the project purpose. Don't omit testing procedures. Don't confuse wants with needs: wants are nice, but they can be very expensive. And often they're unnecessary.

You can update your requirement traceability matrix for the drug approval project to include the requirements that have emerged in the process that you've undertaken. You now have a good foundation for the work you'll be doing.

CLARIFYING A PROJECT'S SCOPE

For any project you obviously want to find out what should be included in the project – and what should not be included. You'll also want to break down the deliverables into activities that you can perform.

What we call the project scope represents the deliverables, and all the work to be completed. And it's derived from the project requirements, it's the major influence on schedule and budget, and the basis for estimating resources, costs, and project duration.

Scope is often represented in a diagram called a work breakdown structure or WBS: this is just a visual way of laying out the project so it's easy to keep track of.

A WBS shows high-level planning decomposed into specific work packages, which you can then use as a guide for estimating resources, costs, and duration.

There's no right or wrong way to structure this work: the point is that you want to represent the work activities in a way that suits your needs.

To start with, you might consider the nature of the drug approval process, and the size of the project, and then organize the work logically. When you know the nature of the work beforehand you might work down from the highest level – or the project – to the major components such as deliverables, product components, or functions. What are the major pieces of work that the project involves?

The lowest level of the WBS is called a work package. Work packages represent anywhere from one day to two weeks' worth of work.

But it really depends on the size and scope of your project. Remember, your goal is to get a clear view of all the work that must go into the project.

Keep breaking down deliverables until you have actions that you can assign time and resource estimates to.

So, "How will I know when a work package is broken down enough?" When a time or resource estimate can be made, you've gone far enough. Breaking the work down too far is often a common mistake, and it wastes your time.

Some experts feel that the duration of work packages should be based on the 8/80 rule. According to this rule, work packages should be typically between 8 and 80 hours of work. Less than 8 hours means you've broken the deliverable down too far. More than 80 hours means that you should break it down further. This is a heuristic rule of thumb that generally applies to projects.

In case this rule doesn't seem to fit, there are some other questions you could ask to determine whether work packages have been broken down far enough.

"Is the product, service, or result verifiable or measurable at this level?" Because you need to be able to apply quality criteria to that deliverable.

If you look at a deliverable and say to yourself, "I would first have to know how long that research is going to take before I can start this particular work?", it's a sign that the deliverable should be broken down further.

You can use your judgment when making these decisions, drawing on your familiarity with the work, the importance of the activity to the success of the project, and what happens if something goes wrong.

The great thing about the WBS is that all other planning documents can be created from it. The WBS will be referred to throughout the project.

But do remember that there is no right or wrong way to structure the work for a project! Three project managers could take the same project and identify completely different components and work packages, and still have organized it appropriately.

Even in organizations that don't use an official WBS, it's still useful to have a representation of all the work required. It could just be shown as an outline: the main thing is that it represents all of the work that you need to accomplish.

SETTING MILESTONES

The task of managing a project can be a long and challenging road, so it's helpful if you have some milestones along the way. Basically, it can be difficult to make progress if you don't have a way to measure progress.

So what exactly are milestones in this context? Well, a milestone is a marker that identifies a significant point or event in a project. Technically it has zero duration, but it sets expectations and signifies progress – and possibly problems – if it's missed or never met.

If a milestone is missed then the team knows that it's behind schedule and needs to figure out what to do to get back on track. Missed milestones can also flag some deeper problems with the project's health and the way it's being managed.

Some project software packages allow milestones to be included, but you can also just create calendar appointments.

Let's say a milestone was set for the first of March to have a document submitted to the FDA for your drug approval project. "Hey, it's March 1, was it submitted? Yes – cool, we're really good. No? uh-oh, why? What happened?"

You'll find it helpful to label milestones as mandatory or optional.

Mandatory milestones are those required by a contract, or essential in some other ways. In the drug approval example, your company is doing the work for itself, but let's say you've engaged an outside contractor to test the drug on humans. The contract specifies that the testing has to be completed by a certain date. If this milestone is missed, it could delay the rest of the project work.

Optional milestones are at the project manager's discretion, and are useful tools for gauging schedule success. A missed optional milestone would not result in a breach of contract – if there was a contract – but it would give the project manager enough time to correct or prevent a problem. Optional milestones can also be used to celebrate success and create enthusiasm for the project. An example might be that test results show that your new drug was effective for a certain disease.

Actually, the drug approval case is a bit different from many others, as its milestones will shadow those that are inherent to the FDA process – animal testing, human testing, and so on. So, optional milestones may not be as important here as in other kinds of projects. Just remember - all projects are unique.

Now let's think about how you should set your milestones. A good idea is just look at the project start and final deliverables, and mark the progress points in between.

"How important is this activity, decision, or event to the overall project completion? What's the likely impact if it isn't met on time or as needed?"

Bear in mind though that milestones shouldn't be overused. They must have meaning and significance. They are the major transition points along the way.

If you miss a milestone, you risk the ability to remain on schedule and within budget, and things can quickly get out of control. You should be able to report the progress of the project to the sponsor at all times. If you can't do this, then the project may lose funding for no other reason except mismanagement – which could have been avoided.

You need to be very careful in setting and monitoring milestones. Missed milestones – or milestones that look like they're about to be missed – need to be addressed immediately.

EXERCISE: GETTING YOUR PROJECT OFF TO A GOOD START

1. Exercise Overview

Effective project planning involves getting vital information. Like, who's supporting your project? What are its purpose and objectives? And what are the risks and constraints? Once you've identified the key project elements, you then need to collect the project requirements, clarify its scope, and establish key milestones.

In this exercise, you'll demonstrate that you can:

- identify the main elements of project
- recognize key stakeholders
- define your project's requirements
- break a project down to define its scope, and
- identify mandatory and optional milestones.

2. Exercise: Get Your Project Started

Question

Suppose you're a production manager for a clothing manufacturer. You've been given the lead on a project to design and sell T-shirts for an upcoming championship final that will display the finalists' official team logos.

Before getting started, what are appropriate questions you should ask to help clarify your understanding of the project?

Options:

1. Who do I ask about the design and distribution budget?
2. How much revenue can we make from these T-shirts?
3. When does the championship final take place?
4. What are the risks of distributing the T-shirt worldwide?
5. Can I assume our graphics team will be available to work on the design?
6. Who'll be held responsible if the T-shirts aren't available 48 hours after the finalists are known?
7. Can I assume that the company stands to make $1 million in profit from the plan?

Answer

Option 1: *This option is correct. Finding out who is sponsoring the project - and who is ultimately providing the project budget - is one of the first things to consider when undertaking a project.*

Option 2: *This option is correct. This question helps define one of the project objectives, and is one that requires a specific and measurable answer. Getting an estimate on revenue can also strengthen the business case to get stakeholder buy-in.*

Option 3: *This option is correct. You need to determine the key dates for your project as these will provide useful checkpoints to monitor progress and to re-estimate factors such as budget and resources.*

Option 4: *This option is correct. Taking into account potential problems, such as logistical issues, is vital in ensuring you come up with effective risk mitigation and contingency plans.*

Option 5: *This option is correct. Initial assumptions about scope, approach, funding, or, as in this case, resources, need to be tested in order to ensure you don't get any last minute surprises that could derail your project.*

Option 6: This option is incorrect. While it's important to consider constraints such as time limitations for your product, the aim of asking clarifying questions is not to find out who'll be accountable if things go wrong. They should instead help you plan your project in more detail.

Option 7: This option is incorrect. In this example, you're making an assumption about a project outcome that should be left to senior management. The assumptions you need to focus on involve project variables such as approach, funding, and scope.

Question

Now consider the stakeholders for the project. Which stakeholders have the most power and interest in the project?

Access the learning aid Identifying Stakeholders on a Project to help you answer the question.

Options:

1. The clothing manufacturer's senior management
2. The clothing manufacturer's supply chain manager
3. The Art Director
4. The T-shirt supplier
5. The rival T-shirt manufacturer

Answer

Option 1: This option is correct. As senior management are bankrolling this project and want regular progress reports, they represent a significant stakeholder for this project.

Option 2: This option is correct. While the supply chain manager doesn't have a strong degree of power in this case, he will have an important impact on the project's success.

Option 3: This option is correct. Although not the main driver for the project, the Art Director is responsible for creating the design, so his output will have a lot influence on its success.

Option 4: *This option is incorrect. As the T-shirt supplier will just need to confirm that they can deliver the quantity required on the dates specified, they require much less management as the key stakeholders.*

Option 5: *This option is incorrect. The rival company will have at most a tangential effect on the outcome of the project, and there is little you can do to manage the competition posed by their products in the run-up to the championship final.*

Question

You've identified senior management to be one of your project's main stakeholders. What is the most appropriate action to take to manage this stakeholder?

Access the learning aid Identifying Stakeholders on a Project to help you answer the question.

Options:

1. Provide reports on project expenses and ask for advice if there are issues with the budget
2. Contact them for authorization on major issues and occasionally inform them of progress
3. Inform them of decisions you've made in relation to budgeting
4. Communicate only when they raise any questions about the project's budget

Answer

Option 1: *This is the correct option. As senior management are highly influential and have a keen interest in making a profit from the project, you'll need to regularly inform of project costings. And because they have control over the budget, you'll need authorization from them if there are any related problems.*

Option 2: *This option is incorrect. This action would be more appropriate if senior management didn't have direct investment in the project. However, as they are sponsoring the project, you'll also need to report* to them frequently to keep them satisfied.

Option 3: *This option is incorrect. Taking this type of action would be more suitable if the stakeholder did not have the authority to make project decisions. In this example though, senior management are the ones who hold the purse strings, and they need to be consulted before you can make any budgeting decisions.*

Option 4: *This option is incorrect. In this case, senior management are sponsoring the project and provide authorization for major decisions, meaning you should report to them regularly, and not just when they raise questions.*

Learning Aid

Identifying Stakeholders on a Project

Purpose: *Use this learning aid to help you answer two practice questions.*

As part of the project plan, you've outlined five stakeholders who might have an input in the project:

- **The clothing manufacturer's senior management** - Senior management have provided a high-level budget of $.5 million for the project. They've made it clear they expect to see a strong return on their investment, and want to know how the project is progressing.
- **The clothing manufacturer's supply chain manager** - You will be cooperating closely with the Supply Chain Manager on all aspects of material costs forecasts, staffing levels to load and unload consignments, and selection of transportation routes. You will be advising him of key delivery dates, which he will need to plan and organize for. Break down
- **The art director** - The Art Director will be alerted immediately when the championship finalists have been announced. He will then be responsible for creating the actual t-shirt design once all trademark issues have been settled. He has a lot of knowledge of and experience in corporate art design wants to make sure he enhances his reputation as well as that of his department by creating

a great design.

- **The T-shirt supplier** - Initially, you will be in contact with the supplier to determine if they can meet the quantity required, and how long it will take for them to deliver the consignments.

- **A rival T-shirt manufacturer** - You are aware that one of your main rivals is also planning to design and distribute t-shirts for the same championship final. You need to consider which retailers they may be targeting, and try to get your product on the shelves before theirs.

Question

As you prepare for the project, you decide to gather the project requirements.

Match each description to the phase it illustrates.

Options:

A. You meet senior executives to discuss key delivery dates for the T-shirts as outlined in the statement of work

B. You organize a brainstorming session with the Art Department to discuss trademark issues, decide on general designs, and narrow down the choice of designs

C. You decide all stakeholders, including senior management and the Art Department, must agree on a specific set of requirements

D. You create a spreadsheet with a list of key deliverables and sales objectives for the T-shirts

Targets:

1. Gather general information about requirements from stakeholders
2. Use different tools and techniques to refine requirements
3. Determine which requirements are priorities

4. Document requirements

Answer

The first phase of the requirements gathering process involves collecting general information about the project, which can be garnered from examining the business case or statement of work with the key stakeholders.

The second phase of requirements gathering consists of defining specific requirements and ranking them according to importance. In this case, a brainstorming session can help get a range different perspectives from stakeholders.

The third stage of the requirements gathering process entails determining how decisions will be made about which ones are in scope. In this case, you want a unanimous decision, as opposed to a majority or a large block of stakeholders agreeing on them.

The final stage is when you document the requirements you've agreed upon in a spreadsheet or matrix. This enables you to associate objectives with each requirement, keep better track of your budget, and help you stay on schedule.

Question

Now that you've gathered key information and identified stakeholders and requirements, it's time to clarify what actually needs to be done. Access the learning aid Clarifying Project Scope and answer the following question.

Which Work Breakdown Structure best defines the work that needs to be carried out for your project to be successful?

Options:

1. WBS A
2. WBS B
3. WBS C

Answer

An appropriate WBS uses a high level description at the top - your project - and then breaks it down into major components. These components are then broken down into packages that typically take between eight and 80 hours to complete.

Option 1: *This is the best option. The top level of WBS A is the project, which is appropriately broken down into two major components - T-Shirt Production and T-Shirt Distribution. These are further broken down into smaller work packages without going into fine details.*

Option 2: *This isn't the best WBS for the project. Although the WBS uses a correct top level description, it omits the major component level where the project is broken down into smaller chunks of work, going directly to work packages. It's important to include the major component level as this will give you a better idea of the deliverables, phases, or functions involved in your project.*

Option 3: *This isn't the best WBS for the project. It uses a work package at the top level, and goes into fine detail as a result of overanalyzing the work package. Each work package at the bottom level will most likely take less than eight hours, meaning it has been broken down too far.*

Learning Aid

Clarifying Project Scope

Purpose: *Use this learning aid to help you answer a practice question.*

Review the Work Breakdown Structure diagrams labeled A, B, and C and answer the associated practice question.

Work Breakdown Structure A	
1.0	Championship T-Shirt
1.1	T-Shirt Production
1.1.1	T-Shirt Design

1.1.2	T-Shirt Supply
1.2	T-Shirt Distribution
1.2.1	Seller Channels
1.2.2	Advertising

Work Breakdown Structure B

1.0	Championship T-Shirt
1.1	T-Shirt Design
1.2	T-Shirt Supply
1.3	Seller Channels
1.4	Advertising

Work Breakdown Structure C

1.0	T-Shirt Design
1.1	Art Department Research
1.1.1	Review five design proposals
1.1.2	Approve final design
1.2	Image Preparation

1.2.1	Submit design to printer
1.2.2	Carry out quality control

Question

You've managed to get a major clothing retailer to sell the Championship final T-shirts internationally. As part of the contract agreement, you need to deliver 50,000 T-shirts to the retailer's warehouses well in advance of the championship final to receive full payment, otherwise your company is liable for a late delivery penalty fee. You'll have one month between knowing who the finalists are and the actual final. It is now two months before the final, and you'd like to set some milestones to gauge the project's progress.

What are appropriate milestones to set in order to manage your project effectively?

Options:

1. T-shirt consignments ready for delivery two weeks before championship final
2. Minimum of 25,000 T-shirts finished within one week of announcement of the finalists
3. Art Department to complete artwork proposals within one week
4. Retailer to have T-shirts on shelves one week before championship final

Answer

Option 1: *This option is correct. As on time delivery of the T-shirts is required by contract, this is a mandatory milestone. One of your company's main objectives - increasing revenues - could also be jeopardized by missing this milestone.*

Option 2: *This option is correct. This is an example of an optional* milestone. Missing this milestone doesn't result in a breach of contract but it does help you gauge the project progress and gives you time to increase production if you're behind the target set.

Option 3: This option is incorrect. Milestones are not work packages or activities; instead, they indicate achievements on a project. In this case, completing T-shirt design proposals is a work package, and does not help you gauge if you can meet the schedule agreed with the retailer.

Option 4: This option is incorrect. This milestone is not relevant to your project. Your major deliverable is to have the T-shirt consignments delivered to the retailer's warehouses in advance of the final, and does not concern how quickly the retailer puts the T-shirts up for sale.

PLAN A BULLETPROOF PROJECT

Wouldn't it be great if you could make your project foolproof? Well, in this course I am going to show you just how to do that.

Once a project has been initiated, it's time to get into more detailed planning. You need to define the work and resources required to meet objectives and complete the project. This course focuses on some core planning concepts related to time, cost, and scope.

You'll learn how to sequence activities to develop a schedule and plan resources. You'll also find out about assessing risks and estimating costs. Let's get started.

Develop Project Plans and Baselines

1. What Happens When?
2. What Resources Do We Need?
3. Assessing Project Risks
4. Estimating Project Costs
5. Exercise: Developing Project Plans

WHAT HAPPENS WHEN?

In any project, a missed deadline or an activity done out of sequence could have a domino effect – for example, the project might deliver late, or cost more. And the one place where there's no room for surprises is during a project.

So let's say you've been assigned to lead a project that involves printing 50,000 t-shirts for a sport event. Wow, that's a lot of t-shirts! Also, each one's going to be sold in a special "collectible" bag. You're going to have to keep on top of quite a few activities and make sure they're completed on schedule! In this case the timing is especially crucial: they're not going to delay the sports event because you haven't printed the t-shirts yet!

So, once you've defined the activities that will help achieve project objectives, and have a general idea of the types resources you need, you must figure out what needs to be done when. So scheduling involves converting the work into sequenced activities.

First, arrange the deliverables or milestones into a logical sequence using a network diagram. It has rectangles for deliverables and arrows showing relationships between them. From this point, a preliminary schedule can be constructed, and from that point a preliminary project cost can be derived.

As well as the relationships between the deliverables, you can see if there are any dependencies between them, and if there are any things that can be done concurrently.

You can also record the relationships in a table like this one, showing the predecessors of each step and possibly an estimate of the duration. It's just another way of looking at the same data, which you may find useful.

If we go back to that network diagram, we can put those estimated durations in place. We'll talk more about durations later.

You'll find that determining the sequence of activities is useful because it shows which activities are independent of each other, and which activities depend on others finishing before they can start.

It also warns the team about which delays could potentially affect the project completion date. It identifies activities that are critical to maintaining the schedule, as well as the relationships between the activities. If the bag production package is delayed for example, the entire project will be delayed.

I've used quite a bit of scheduling terminology here, so let's take a moment to go over some of these terms – and you'll be using them yourself before long.

An activity is the work required to complete a work package. If planning was done at the deliverable level, each activity represents a portion of the work needed to complete that deliverable.

An activity sequence is the logical order of those activities. For example, t-shirt design precedes t-shirt printing.

Multiple activities that can be done during the same time frame are said to be parallel. For example, advertising copy and art work can be done at the same time as t-shirts and bags are being designed.

A predecessor is an activity that must begin or end before another activity can begin or end.

The successor is an activity that follows a predecessor activity. This is also known as a dependent activity.

Milestones are markers that show a point in time – they have zero duration because no actual work is done here.

In some cases – though it's not as relevant in the t-shirt printing example – the longest path on the diagram will show the overall time line for the project. The activities along this path are the critical ones that, if delayed or not done, will put the whole project at risk.

Now that I've provided you with these concepts, you'll have a better idea to figure out how "what happens when."

WHAT RESOURCES DO WE NEED?

Determining resource requirements is critical to successful time and cost management. Let's return to the t-shirt printing project you've been asked to manage. What resources will you need in terms of people, material, equipment, facilities, and money to produce the 50,000 shirts you need?

You'll start by listing the project deliverables, and then identify and sequence the activities required to produce them. A work breakdown structure, or WBS, will help with this. It's a kind of picture of this whole scope that lets you see what's going on.

As you draw up your plan, you'll add details. Each activity requires resources. For example, the actual printing of the t-shirt will require plain t-shirts, ink, screen printing equipment, and labor.

You'll find it useful to describe the resources for each activity in terms of type, quantity, required skill sets, and team roles.

Types of resources come first. This includes physical resources such as computers and human resources or people. It's the starting point for budgeting and scheduling. In the example, you might list plain t-shirts, printing equipment, ink, and the people who will do the work.

Next you'll determine the quantity of each resource. This is important for scheduling and estimating costs. Sometimes not enough resources are available, so the project manager will propose to extend the schedule, or budget for overtime. You might calculate that you'll need six people for this job and then need to ask for more people. For the design and the quantity of t-shirts, let's say that 125 gallons of ink will be required.

To make sure that you have the right people, you'll define the skill sets for each activity. If certain skill sets are not available in the employee pool, you might bring in a contractor, provide skill training, or add time to the schedule. Let's imagine that the skills are available in-house for the printing job.

So now you have to look at roles on the project team, and whether the people identified will be available when needed. You need to consider vacation times, leave schedules, and other work obligations, and other projects. Perhaps one of your key people will be on vacation for part of the planned time. How are you gonna address this?

As part of your planning, you'll assign responsibilities to each activity. You might use what's called a RACI chart – this stands for responsible, accountable, consult, and inform. A person or group that does the work is responsible; a person that approves the work is accountable; someone who has relevant information will be consulted; and anyone who needs to be updated will be informed.

A RACI chart helps to ensure that activities are not forgotten, and to clarify roles and responsibilities. This means that no one will be able to say "That's not my responsibility." You'll have it all worked out in advance, so everyone will know their responsibilities.

ASSESSING PROJECT RISKS

Famous last words: "What could possibly go wrong?" The reality is lots of things could! And if they do, you'll need to know how to respond. You're still working on that t-shirt project, and you have an unmovable deadline – they've got be done before the sports event.

Risks are events that can affect a project's outcome. For project management purposes, negative risks are called threats and are likely to delay the schedule, increase costs, or impact the scope. Positive risks are called opportunities and may allow you to gain time or earn extra money. Our focus here is on negative risks.

Basically, risk management has two central roles – reducing uncertainty about identifying risks, and determining the appropriate responses for unavoidable risks. These roles will enable you to eliminate some of the negative outcomes and take advantage of positive outcomes if a risk event occurs. Now we're going to look at a basic risk analysis process.

First, identifying risks involves determining which risks might affect the project, and documenting them. A common technique is to review project documentation. Comparing the scope and schedule to the contract can uncover obvious risks. Evaluating the likelihood of resources being available and activities finishing on time can uncover threats to the due date or a likely cost overrun. Evaluating requirements, workflow, and processes can uncover threats to the performance of the final product or service. So, basically, you'll need to take a good look at your plan to find any flaws in it. These are the initial items that are captured in a risk register.

Once threats have been identified, the next stage is to assess their probability and impact. Threats with a high probability and a high impact on schedule or budget need to be monitored closely, while threats with a low probability and low impact may simply be accepted, as in the diagram plotting impact and probability.

The third stage, once a risk has been identified and assessed, is to plan a response. There are four categories of negative risk responses: avoid, transfer, mitigate, and accept.

First of all, you can avoid a risk by changing the due date, adding funds to the budget, or removing a scope item to avoid an impact on time, cost, or quality. Alternatively, you can replace the risky item with a less risky version.

In the t-shirt project, the person in charge of the screen printing machinery has told you that it may not be up to such an intensive job; it's quite old and needs expensive new parts. You could choose to buy the new parts, which would add to the budget.

Another option is to transfer a risk by outsourcing, buying insurance, or paying for a warranty – this shifts the negative impact, along with responsibility for its management, to a third party. This reduces the risk only if the third party though is more capable.

In the t-shirt project you could hire another company, which has ultramodern equipment, to do the actual printing.

You can mitigate a risk by working to reduce the probability or impact, adding more resources, overlapping activities that should be done in parallel, running more tests, or finding a less expensive alternative.

For example, you might decide to print fewer t-shirts per day, hence decreasing the strain on the printer. This would mean that the time required for other activities would have to be reduced, as the project must be completed before the sports event.

When you accept a risk, you do nothing, or you add money to the budget to pay for the issue if it occurs. Some risks are so small and easily dealt with that it's is not economical to spend time developing a risk response.

Perhaps you do some research and accept expert advice that the printer will in fact be up to the job it's facing. All risk responses are captured on the risk register.

Once the responses have been identified, any costs related to them should also be included in the budget. These costs are referred to as risk reserves. In some projects the risk reserves are added to the work package costs, and then aggregated into the overall time-phased cost baseline. They may also be accumulated into a single budget line item identified as a risk reserve.

Risk owners are people who should be identified to monitor the risk and roll out the response. Also, risk triggers should be documented so that the risk owner can roll the response into place before it's too late.

It's important that risks be monitored throughout the duration of the project. When a risk has passed it should be marked as such, and when a risk does occur, the effectiveness of the response should be documented. This way, the organization can improve its risk management techniques and do better the next time. And you'll be able to learn from any mistakes you might have made.

ESTIMATING PROJECT COSTS

Anyone who's done home repairs knows that no matter how much money you budget, it never seems to be enough. Your t-shirt printing project has a budget of half a million dollars. Seems like an awful lot of money, but will it really be enough? To find out, you're going to need to do some checks and some calculations.

Projects are generally authorized with a specific budget, like yours has been. After the scope and schedule have been created, the project manager needs to establish a budget or verify that the budget can be met.

So, if the scope of work, the cost of resources and materials, and the duration of the schedule aren't in line with the vision of the project when it was funded, there is clearly going to be a problem. You, as the leader for the project, need to identify any discrepancies as early as possible so that adjustments can be made that will allow the project to meet the scope, schedule, and budget, and will deliver the t-shirts in time to coincide with the sports event.

Basically, your cost-related activities during the planning phase will involve estimating costs and determining a cost baseline for the project.

You'll then add risk response estimates – called risk reserves – to the cost estimates. This is just extra money that you set aside for the risks you've identified and assessed – there's always the possibility that something will go wrong!

After you've worked out the cost baseline, it can be compared with the authorized project budget, and discrepancies can be noted. The project manager has the flexibility to talk to the customer, if there is one, or the sponsor, and a solution can be agreed upon – for example, we might change the scope, source cheaper materials, or find another way to reduce costs. Alternatively, the sponsor might suggest increasing the budget.

Of all the tools and techniques for determining a project budget, cost aggregation is the one you typically use first when establishing a cost baseline. This enables you to determine the cost of each work package that you've identified during planning.

Let's say that the project activities you identified are shown in this flow chart. To aggregate costs correctly, you'll begin by estimating the cost of each activity as accurately as possible and assigning dates to each cost estimate based on the project schedule.

There are two easy methods for arriving at cost estimates: parametric and analogous.

Parametric estimating sounds more difficult than it really is.

On your t-shirts project Let's say you need 93 days of labor at an average cost of $300 per day – you begin with an overall resource cost of $27,900.

Analogous estimating is simply looking at past projects or historical information and modifying it if necessary. For example, a recent project in your company involved printing 20,000 t-shirts and cost $200,000, so you can multiply the cost by 2.5 to get a cost for 50,000 t-shirts. Analogous estimates are not always reliable – they may not take account of economies of scale, for example – but they're a great place to start.

Other cost estimates come from fixed price contracts. For example, you may have ordered 125 gallons of screen printing ink at $200 per gallon, giving a cost of $25,000. You also have 50,000 t-shirts at $4.50 each and a packaging cost of $25,000.

Once you've estimated the cost of each work activity, you'll add them all together, along with the risk reserves, to come up with your planned project costs. Let's say that you've also allocated $150,000 for advertising, and you're adding a 10% risk contingency. As you can see, your cost baseline is now coming in very close to the authorized budget ceiling, of $500,000.

If the cost baseline isn't accurately established, you won't be able to monitor and control actual project costs. So it's very important that you verify the cost baseline that you've developed.

The best way to do this is to ask yourself some questions.

"Were the costs correctly aggregated at the activity, work package, and/or the project level?"

"Were the contingency reserves included?"

Finally, you can ask yourself, "Were the correct dates assigned to each cost estimate based on the project schedule?"

If the answer to all of these is "yes," you can now move forward confidently with your project.

EXERCISE: DEVELOPING PROJECT PLANS

1. Exercise Overview

Once a project has been initiated, it's time to get into more detailed planning. As project lead, you must now define the work and resources required to meet objectives and complete the project. The plans you develop will help create the scope, cost, and schedule baselines to be used throughout the project.

In this exercise, you'll demonstrate that you can

- identify resources for a project
- use a task sequence diagram to help develop a project schedule
- take steps to identify and mitigate risks, and
- determine how to establish a cost baseline

2. Exercise: Developing Project Plans

Question

You work for a publisher of school books and learning materials. Your current project is to organize your company's exhibition stall at a teachers' conference. The stall will feature an onscreen demo of the company's digital products.

What are appropriate considerations for the resources required for this project?

Access the learning aid Conference Stall Project and examine the section "Project Description" to help you answer this question.

Options:

1. Determining the quantity of marketing materials you'll need
2. Finding out who in the IT department will be available to help with the demo
3. Figuring out how long it will take to create a demo for the flagship product so you can assign the right number of resources
4. Calculating the costs of the conference and submitting a budget to your manager
5. Assessing project risks so you don't miss your schedule

Answer

Option 1: *This option is correct. Identify the types of resources required and also quantify exactly how many of each you'll need.*

Option 2: *This option is correct. Identify the appropriate human resources and define the skill sets required to perform each activity. This will impact on your budget.*

Option 3: *This option is correct. As well as physical resources, list human resources too. You need to do this before you can create a project team.*

Option 4: *This option is incorrect. This is not a resource consideration. You have to work out resources before you can consider costs.*

Option 5: *This option is incorrect. Assessing project risks comes later on in planning.*

Question

Having made plans for resources, you now create a project diagram to help you schedule.

Which statements most accurately describe what the diagram tells you with respect to scheduling the project?

Access the learning aid Conference Stall Project and examine the section "Sequencing Activities" to help you answer this question.

Options:

1. If the creation of educational content or printing of marketing materials is delayed, it could affect the entire schedule
2. The preparation of the laptops, projector and screen can be scheduled independently of any other actions
3. The design of marketing materials should be scheduled to start after the educational content is written
4. The entire project will take four days

Answer

Option 1: *This option is correct. These activities are on Path 2, which is the most critical path, since it is the longest. This means that other paths can afford to be slightly delayed, but this one can't.*

Option 2: *This option is incorrect. The preparation of the laptops, projector and screen depends on the completion of the animation demo.*

Option 3: *This option is correct. Before you can design and print marketing materials, you must write the educational materials. This means you must schedule enough time for the writing of materials and coordinate it with the start of the design of the marketing materials.*

Option 4: *This option is incorrect. In fact, the project, if it runs on time, will take five days.*

Question

Having created a schedule, you now assess the risks associated with the creation of the stall. Match each risk assessment step to the example that best illustrates it. Not all examples may match to a step.

Access the learning aid Conference Stall Project and examine the section "Identifying Risks" to help you answer this question.

Options:

    A.   Identify the risk

    B.   Assess the risk's impact

    C.   Determine an appropriate response

Targets:

1. You propose bringing a second designer into the project, budget permitting
2. You realize only one designer is doing the stand artwork and material design
3. You figure that the designer could get caught up with the creation of stand artwork and banners, and then start work late on the brochures and posters
4. You change the due date for the printed marketing materials

Answer

By bringing in a second designer to work on the printed materials, you are planning an appropriate response to mitigate the risk and avoid any delays.

The first thing to do when assessing risk is look for any possible risks. You have identified a possible risk, with one designer scheduled to do two jobs.

You assess the probability and impact of the risk. Since the two jobs overlap in the schedule, with only one person dedicated to both, there's a high risk one may be delayed. A delay in either could mean you don't have the materials ready for the conference, which means this risk is high impact. You must respond to it.

This is not an appropriate action to take. It is not feasible to change the due date for the completion of printed materials, since you can't change the date of the conference.

Question

There's a slight risk that the animation company won't have the demo ready for the first conference.

What is the most appropriate response to plan for this risk?

Access the learning aid Conference Stall Project and examine the section "Identifying Risks" to help you answer this question.

Options:

1. Avoid the risk. Don't create a demo at all.
2. Transfer the negative impact of the risk to a third party. Ask the conference organizers for a money-back warranty should your stall not be ready.
3. Mitigate the risk. Hire a second animation company to take on the animation development.
4. Accept the risk. Ask the animation company for a guarantee on timely delivery, and monitor their progress.

Answer

Option 1: Avoidance isn't the most appropriate response. The risk that the animation company won't deliver is low. Plus, the animation is an important part of the display.

Option 2: This isn't the most appropriate response. The conference organizers are unlikely to issue a refund. There is no third party to whom the risk can be transferred: your company must absorb the risk.

Option 3: Mitigating the risk isn't the most appropriate response. Hiring a second animation company doesn't make sense. The risk of being late with the demo is too low to take such an action. You'd be spending twice the amount of money for the demo.

Option 4: This is the most appropriate response. The animation company has a good track record, so even though the impact of the risk may be high, the probability is not. The most appropriate action is to *accept the risk, but you can ask for a guarantee, and check in with them periodically to see how they're progressing.*

Question

Next, you aggregate costs for the project.

What did you neglect to do in establishing the cost baseline?

Access the learning aid Conference Stall Project and examine the section "Aggregating Costs" to help you answer this question.

Options:

1. Correctly aggregate costs at each subproject level
2. Include contingency reserves
3. Calculate the total cost correctly
4. Assign appropriate dates based on the schedule
5. Calculate parametric costs correctly

Answer

Option 1: *This option is incorrect. You correctly calculated the total for the conference-booking subproject at $3,885. And you correctly calculated the total for the assembly of materials subproject at $4,095.*

Option 2: *This option is incorrect. You included contingency reserves of 5% for all amounts and total.*

Option 3: *This is the correct option. You didn't add the contingency reserves. The total cost should be $9,240.*

Option 4: *This option is incorrect. You've included the start dates for each activity. This helps you align your cost estimates with the schedule for the project.*

Option 5: *This option is incorrect. It costs $100 to print each of three marketing items, which works out as $300 in total. The animation company charges $500 per day, and will take three days to complete the animation, which works out as $1,500. You've calculated both of these parametric costs correctly.*

Learning Aid

Conference Stall Project

Purpose: *Use this learning aid to help you answer practice questions.*

Project Description

You work for a publisher of school books and learning materials and you're organizing an exhibition stall at various teachers' conferences around the country over two weeks in May. As well as school books, the stall will provide access to an online portal where teachers can view e-books and your company's flagship interactive digital activities, which you hope to be a major selling point for teachers.

The stall requires branded backdrops, banners, and signage. Marketing materials, such as brochures and posters containing curriculum-specific content, will also be available to teachers. The star of the show will be a large screen displaying a three-minute animated demo of some of the portal and digital features. The laptops, projector, and screen will need to be configured and set up by IT personnel.

Sequencing Activities

Here is a sequence diagram you are using to describe the project.

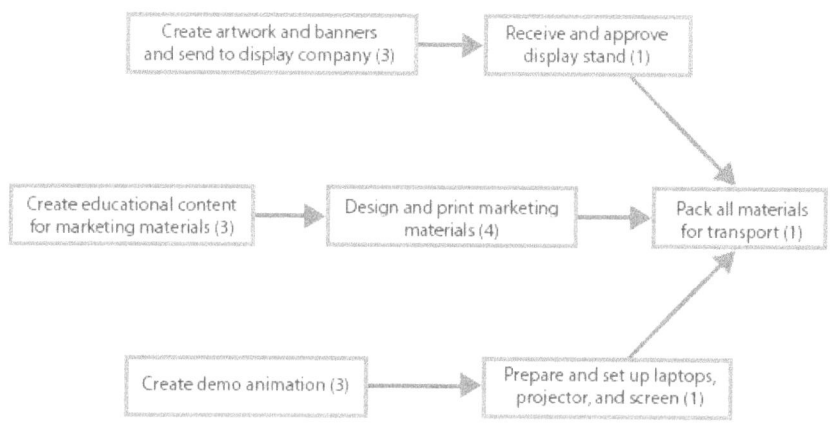

Sequencing diagram

Here is a table describing the activities, durations, and predecessor relationships of the Conference Stall project.

	Activity	Duration (days)	Predecessor
Path 1	Create artwork and banners and send to display company	3	—
Path 1	Receive and approve display stand	1	Create artwork and banners and send to display company

Path 2	Create educational content for marketing materials	3	—
Path 2	Design and print marketing materials	4	Create educational content for marketing materials
Path 3	Create demo animation	3	—
Path 3	Prepare and set up laptops, projector, and screen	1	Create demo animation
Path 3	Pack all materials for transport	1	Receive and approve display stand; Design and print marketing materials; Prepare and set up laptops, projector, and screen

Identifying Risks

You identify some possible risks with the project:

- One designer is assigned to do both the artwork for the stand and for the printed materials. These tasks must start at the same time.
- The demo of the flagship products is being created by an animation company, which has a good track record and has committed to your delivery date. For technical reasons, the configuring and setup of the laptop and projector, which takes a full day, can't begin until the animation is delivered. A delay of one day would mean having to do this setup at the conference, which is undesirable. And a delay by more than a day would mean having to go to the conference without it, which would

be out of the question.

Aggregating Costs

Here is a table of aggregated costs you established for the project. You have set contingency reserves at 5%. The booth must be hired at least a month in advance. You have then scheduled eight days for the creation of the stand and materials, with the conference starting on the morning of August 19. There are three different items to be printed: it costs $100 for each item. The animation company charges $500 per day, and will take three days to complete the animation.

Cost baseline for conference stall project				
Work package	Start date	Cost	Contingency reserves	Total
Booth space hire and insurance	July 15	$3,700	$185	$3,885
Conference booking complete		$3,700	$185	$3,885
Create educational content for marketing materials	Aug 13	$400	$20	$420
Create demo animation	Aug 13	$1,500	$75	$1,575
Design marketing materials	Aug 14	$1,200	$60	$1,260
Hire display stand	Aug 17	$1,200	$60	$1,260
Print marketing	Aug 18	$300	$15	$315

materials				
Projector and screen hire	Aug 18	$900	$45	$945
All materials complete		**$5,100**	**$255**	**$5,355**
Total cost		**$8,800**		**$8,800**

COMPLETE YOUR PROJECT ON-TIME AND ON-BUDGET

As a project progresses, you need to respond promptly to any changes, adjusting as necessary to meet new demands. Controlling a project means comparing actual performance with planned performance, analyzing variances, evaluating possible alternatives, and recommending appropriate corrective action as needed.

In this course, you'll learn about some key aspects of controlling your project.

There are always going to be some issues and difficulties that you'll encounter during a project. Just be aware that you're not alone, and that there are proven techniques for overcoming these obstacles. We're going to cover some useful strategies that are easy to understand and to apply. Let's get started.

Control and Close Your Project

1. Controlling the Project Schedule
2. Controlling Project Costs
3. Responding to Changes
4. Closing Your Project
5. Exercise: Controlling and Closing a Project

CONTROLLING THE PROJECT SCHEDULE

Let's say that you've been assigned to manage the production of a series of illustrated children's books, as well as a website and software. The schedule's going to be quite complex, with a lot of different activities – it's important that you'll be able to stay on top of it!

How are you going to achieve this? Controlling a schedule means measuring and monitoring project activities so that corrective actions can be taken when necessary. One of the key ways to maintain control is to review and update the schedule on a regular basis.

For example, activities that have been completed during the current week should be updated to show a completed status. The remaining activities should be reviewed to determine the focus for the current week. If any activities are behind schedule, decisions should be made immediately on how to get back on track.

As the person responsible for the project, you'll have to be aware of signs that the project is heading for trouble. If the number of late activities keeps increasing each week, for example, or the planned versus actual variances gets bigger, these warning signs should not be ignored. Find out the causes! You may need to adjust the baseline plan to reflect current project realities or re-plan activity durations.

Luckily, there are some techniques that will help you control schedule variance. One of these is schedule compression. This means shortening the duration of the schedule without changing the scope. There are two ways of doing this; they're known as fast tracking and crashing.

Fast tracking means rearranging relationships between activities to shorten the schedule. Instead of completing one activity and then starting the next activity, they're partially carried out simultaneously.

So let's say that you originally hired six freelance writers and six freelance artists: the writers were to produce one book each and the artists were to start work when the writing was finished. Halfway through the three-month writing window, four of the writers have written much less than what was scheduled. You may feel that it's necessary to get the artists involved at this point, in order to gain some time.

Fast tracking will only work if activities can be overlapped to shorten the project duration. You should bear in mind that it threatens the quality of the deliverable, and may result in rework and increased risk.

Let's say that one of the artists is in charge of establishing and maintaining a common style and visual vocabulary. She feels that this will be more difficult if the books are still being written while the art is under way. Time may be saved at this stage, but some of the illustrations may need to be modified at a later stage – which will take time, and money!

If you do decide to use fast tracking, it is easily done with project management software. When activities are added into the software they'll have a start date, a finish date, duration, and predecessor and successor activities. This links them together. The activities can be modified so as to have "lead time" – in other words, to start earlier than the predecessor's finish date. The software will display the activities as overlapping – as in the writing and artwork example.

Another technique you could consider, in terms of compressing your schedule, is crashing. This simply means adding more resources to an activity in order to complete it more quickly. It costs more money and does not guarantee an earlier completion date.

For example, in your project you could hire extra writers in an effort to get the writing completed on time, but this could also lead to problems.

You need to beware of diminishing returns: an increased level of effort does not necessarily lead to an increased level of output. In other words, you can assign more resources to a project, and it may help get things back on track, but be careful that you don't bring in too many new resources. Any productivity gains may not be worth the extra cost of their wages, the hours it may take to train and support them, and the increased potential for error and conflict that may result.

In your book project, you may risk alienating the existing writers if you bring in new ones – which probably wouldn't benefit the project.

So, the most feasible option to get the project back on track is to involve more team members, or to ask the ones who are currently involved to work more quickly.

Every situation will be different – what's certain is that you'll need to review your options carefully and think about what's likely to give the best outcome.

CONTROLLING PROJECT COSTS

You're managing the production of a children's book, and the software for a client. It's a complicated task, and clearly it's crucial that you do not allow costs to get out of hand! Let's look at some pointers to help you control your costs.

The good news is that collecting information about costs and schedule performance isn't as difficult as you might think! It's a matter of figuring out a few key factors – the estimated cost for the activities, and the percent complete from performance information and status reports. You'll have your invoices and receipts, so you'll know the actual costs. Now you just need to put those factors together so you can tell if you're over budget.

Making calculations can be intimidating, but if you give it a try, you'll find that it's not that hard.

The good thing is, you can work everything out before you've spent all the money. That way, you'll know which changes need to be made while you still have funding, and when to make them. In project management terms, what we're discussing here is called earned value, and it's really as simple as the math you learned in third grade.

First of all – what should you monitor? You need to assess the project's financial performance by comparing the actual expenditures with what you planned. A typical cost report gives expenditures for the current performance period and from the beginning of the project for different levels of activities. It includes the total funds budgeted for each activity in the performance period, the cumulative funds budgeted to date for each activity, and the total budget for each activity.

Next – how do you monitor? Earned value management, or EVM, is a useful way to identify areas you should keep an eye on for possible current problems or potential future problems.

EVM involves measuring and monitoring three key performance dimensions.

Planned value, or PV, is the amount of the budget allocated for a specific activity.

Earned value, or EV, is the actual value of work completed so far, based on the budgeted funds assigned to that work. So, if an activity valued at $600 is 50% complete, the earned value for this activity is $300.

[A definition for Earned value (EV) is displayed: The measure of work performed, expressed in terms of the budget authorized for that work. In other words, the value of the work actually completed so far, based upon the budget.]

Actual cost, or AC, is the total cost actually incurred up to a specific time.

Once you've calculated the planned value, earned value, and actual cost for the project, you can determine exactly where the project stands in relation to the cost baseline you set during planning. Any departure from this is known as a variance. Let's look at your book software in these terms.

Each activity should have an estimated cost. For example, paying six writers $50 an hour for eight 40-hour weeks comes to $96,000. This is the planned value, or PV.

Multiplying the planned value by the percent complete will indicate the earned value, or EV. If the work is 50% complete, then $96,000 × 0.5 = $48,000. In other words, $48,000 worth of work has been completed.

But maybe the writers have actually taken 5 weeks to complete

50% of the work instead of the 4 weeks as planned. So the actual costs are calculated as 6 writers × $50 × 200 hours, which equals $60,000.

Now, cost variance, or CV, is the difference between what a project has earned to date and what it has cost. This can be viewed as a formula. The writers have completed $48,000 worth of work for $60,000. The negative sign before the $12,000 is important because it indicates that the activity is $12,000 over budget.

This can also be expressed as a percent, in which case it's called a cost performance index, or CPI.

To get the CPI, we divide the earned value, or EV, by the actual cost, or AC. This is a critical EVM metric because it tells you how a project is really performing in terms of costs. A CPI value higher than 1 indicates that a project is earning more than is being spent. A value lower than 1 – such as 0.8 – indicates that the project is underperforming, in this case at an 80% rate.

The earned value technique can be carried out after the project has been in progress for a period of time, and gives you more flexibility to find solutions.

So, in this case, you could analyze why the activity is taking longer than planned. Are the writers working too slowly? Can people be incentivized to work faster? Was there a difficult issue early on that may have been corrected? Is there a steep learning curve? Was the estimate wrong in the beginning? There's certainly plenty to think about, but at least when you know there are problems, you can start to address them.

RESPONDING TO CHANGES

You're deep into your project to produce six different children's books and associated software for a client. It's very likely that the client – or some other stakeholder – will request changes in the course of the project. Will this throw you off balance? It doesn't have to, not if you know how to deal with changes.

Because changes occur so often in projects, handling change well can be the key to success. Documenting change requests and their status can eliminate unnecessary work, and will help to ensure that the project meets requirements on time and on budget.

Uncontrolled changes are those that aren't identified or accepted, but are simply worked in. These can be detrimental for a project because they can bloat the scope, take time, cost money, and sometimes even break functionality that already was working.

For example, you've hired six freelance writers to write the six books independently. The client suggested that all six should collaborate on each book, to ensure "consistency of tone." You feel this is a recipe for disaster!

The term for uncontrolled changes is scope creep, and it's a common occurrence in projects of all sizes. Change can be a corrective action, a preventative action, or to repair defects.

Imagine that your client has decided to give the books some new characters, in addition to the original characters. Or, the website has to go live two weeks earlier than originally planned. You can see how changes like these might seriously impact a project's schedule and budget.

Also, everyone on the team has to understand the need to bring changes to your attention before making them. Make sure there's a system for requesting and documenting changes – this could be as easy as sending an e-mail using a change template, or making an entry in a change request spreadsheet.

Some of the writers may have noticed inconsistencies in the way characters are described in the brief. It's important that these are brought to your attention so that they can be resolved centrally, rather than having the writers independently making incompatible changes.

Many non-project managers who get assigned to lead a project won't formalize a change management process. But they can still learn from these guidelines and take action informally by talking through changes with the project team, evaluating them against the requirements, getting buy-in from the necessary people, adjusting the project plan, and so on. The principles are the same.

So what are the guidelines for responding to change requests?

First, determine who initiated the request and what type of change it asks for. You also need to understand the factors that have led to the request – customer demands, changes in legislation, technical difficulties, or many others.

Second, you should assess what impact the change could have on scope, quality, schedule, and cost. Suppose the change you're considering pushes out the scheduled completion date. That means you'll need resources longer than expected and this will cost the customer more. Involve key people, like stakeholders and project team members.

Next, decide whether the change should go ahead. To help you do this, you need to ask yourself whether making the change will increase or decrease the chances of successful project completion while still meeting the project objectives. For example, your project's software developer may have suggested using a different platform to produce the artwork for the books and the website. What effect would this have on the project?

Finally, document your decision – update the scope baseline, schedule, or other project information so that everything is laid out clearly. Documenting changes to scope will make it easier for you to know whether or not the requirements will be completed on time and on budget.

The very act of collecting change requests will help the organization with future project planning. An exceptionally large number of changes may indicate that key stakeholders were not identified early on, or requirements were not gathered effectively. Lessons can be learned from this for future projects.

Here are some mistakes that people often make – and that you should now know how to avoid: not to track changes; not to communicate the need for change management; allowing people to make modifications without seeking approval; and carrying out unapproved changes that break features that already work, or that override the customer or sponsor's wishes.

If you avoid these pitfalls and apply the principles outlined here, you'll be well on the way to a smooth system of change management and a successful project completion.

CLOSING YOUR PROJECT

When you started your project to produce children's books and software, the end seemed like a long way away. But it'll come! You have to know how to close your project.

Projects have various types of outcome.

In the case of your project, the product will be transferred into the hands of an external customer. Your team will likely hand over the support function to a customer service department or something similar within the organization.

In other cases, a project's result may be transferred internally to be supported by operations.

Alternatively the result may be transferred externally or internally, but kicks off a new project to complete any outstanding issues.

Some projects are canceled before they are completed, for whatever reason.

It's a good idea to perform a few activities when a project is closing. For example, regardless of how the project ends, some project closure meetings may be appropriate. These have a number of purposes.

First, you can gain the customer's acceptance and communicate whether or not there will be future interactions. Is your client thinking about further projects that could use your expertise that the team has demonstrated in this one?

Having done that, you can inform your team of the outcome and communicate the next steps. Congratulate and thank the team – including the freelance writers and artists you've hired – for their hard work. Regardless of the outcome, they need closure. Discuss lessons learned – what went well, and what should be repeated next time? What didn't go so well, and how can the next project be improved?

Also, talk to the sponsor about his or her opinion of the project outcome – and what can be done to improve the way projects are run in the future.

At the close of a project there'll be some administrative closure activities that you'll need to attend to.

You should ensure that all the necessary paperwork is completed and archived – including customer or sponsor sign-offs, finalized project files, and so on.

Any formal procedures that are required by your organization or the contract should be completed as directed.

You'll need to gather lessons learned and archive project information for future use by your organization. For example, you might compile the original project plan, the cost budget, and the project schedule. These may save your company from having to "reinvent the wheel" at some point in the future when a similar project is undertaken.

Also, if a project was not completed, it's critical to document all the information about it in case it's reopened or a similar project is started at a later date.

If the project is canceled or closed early, it's important that you investigate the reasons why – a change in business focus, technology, or legislation; changes in customer demands or in the market or business environment; or the company may have needed resources to respond to a more urgent issue.

You should also give feedback. If team-mates gained any new skills or certifications, or showed leadership capabilities, their personnel records should be updated so that their careers may be advanced.

On the other hand, if teammates underperformed, they should be told immediately so they know where they need to improve. Feedback meetings should be private; they should give specific examples for improvement, and when possible, they should be done in person.

Once the meetings have been completed and it is certain that no more work will be performed, the resources should be released.

You'll need to be aware of the possible adverse outcomes of projects. For example, the contract isn't closed, and your company doesn't get paid for its work, even though it has spent its own money on freelance writers and artists. Or the customer never signs off on the project, perhaps expressing vague dissatisfaction with the deliverables. Or resources are released, the team breaks up, and then the customer decides that they want a change. There's no one left to do it!

Or maybe the administrative closure doesn't happen – the project drags on forever with some work trickling in, or none at all, but the resources can't be diverted to other projects, and employees lose confidence in the organization or quit. Or lessons learned aren't gathered, and the organization never learns systematically from its successes or mistakes.

Of course, all these possible negative scenarios can be avoided or minimized if you apply the principles that you've been learning to the running and the closure of your project. Good luck!

EXERCISE: CONTROLLING AND CLOSING A PROJECT

1. Exercise Overview

As a project progresses, you need to respond promptly to any changes and take action to control the budget and schedule. Once the project has ended, there are also administrative tasks to do.

In this exercise, you'll get to practice what you've learned about schedule and budget control, and how to manage change and project closure.

This involves the following activities:
- deciding what actions will keep the project on schedule
- deciding if an activity is over or under budget
- responding to a change that comes up, and
- effectively closing a project.

2. Exercise: Control and Close a Project

Case Study: Question 1 of 4

Scenario

For your convenience, the case study is repeated with each question.

Your company, an energy provider, is working on a project to install wind turbines for a commercial customer. You're leading a team of 10 engineers, mechanics, and general construction employees. The project has an estimated completion date of six months and a budget of $23 million.

Answer the following questions in order.

Question

Two months into the project, it's time to start laying the foundation for the turbines. However the report on the subsoil analysis hasn't come back yet, and the project is at risk of falling behind.

Which actions can you take to help in this situation?

Options:

1. Begin the assembly of the turbines while the team waits for the report
2. Put more workers on the foundation task than were originally planned
3. Hire three more contractors to begin installing the turbines on the date that was approved in the original schedule
4. Take a week to train more of the existing construction personnel on how to install the turbines while you wait for the subsoils report

Answer

Option 1: *This is a correct option. This is an example of fast tracking, which is rearranging predecessor relationships to shorten the schedule. Instead of completing one activity completely and then starting the next activity, they are carried out simultaneously.*

Option 2: *This is a correct option. Crashing would be appropriate in this case since once the subsoils report comes back, you'll be behind schedule for building the foundation, and putting extra workers on that task should help pull in the schedule.*

Option 3: *This choice is incorrect. This is an example of crashing, which means adding more resources to an activity in an effort to complete it more quickly. In this case, crashing the turbine installation task would bring the project end date in, but it may not have the ori-*

ginal start date. Once the subsoil report is available, the start dates for all subsequent tasks will need to be revised.

Option 4: *This choice is incorrect. This is an example of fast tracking. However, it is not being applied appropriately. Taking time out of the schedule now to train personnel on a task that can't be accomplished right now is a waste of time and won't get the schedule back on track.*

Case Study: Question 2 of 4

Scenario

For your convenience, the case study is repeated with each question.

Your company, an energy provider, is working on a project to install wind turbines for a commercial customer. You're leading a team of 10 engineers, mechanics, and general construction employees. The project has an estimated completion date of six months and a budget of $23 million.

Answer the following questions in order.

Question

Your team is finally ready to start building the foundation for the turbines. You want to know whether the foundation task is running over or under budget. You have calculated some of the values already:

PV = $52,000
EV = $43,200
AC = $50,400

Is this project activity over budget?

Use the job aid Monitoring Your Budget to access the earned value management formulas you'll need to answer this question.

Options:

1. Yes, the negative cost variance value of $7,200 indicates that the activity is over budget
2. No, since the earned value is less than the planned value

3. Yes, since the CPI is calculated as 1.17
4. No, the CPI of 86% indicates that the project is under budget

Answer

Option 1: This is the correct option. Cost variance is calculated by subtracting the actual costs from the earned value. In this case, $43,200 - $50,400 = $-7,200, indicating that the project is over budget by $7,200.

Option 2: This option is incorrect. Planned value doesn't come into play when calculating cost variance or CPI. You need to subtract actual cost from earned value to get the cost variance.

Option 3: This option is incorrect. You seem to have done the calculation backwards, by dividing EV into AC. The correct CPI would be 0.86, which would be 43,200 divided by 50,400. Since the CPI is less than 1, we know the project is over budget.

Option 4: This option is incorrect. You calculate it by dividing the actual costs by the earned value - in this case, 43,200 divided by 50,400 equals 0.86. Since it is less than 1, we know the project is over budget.

Job Aid

Monitoring Your Budget

Purpose: *Use this job aid to help you monitor costs on your project.*

Key terms

Earned Value Management

Involves measuring and monitoring three key performance dimensions: planned value, earned value, and actual cost.

Planned value

Earned value

Earned value, or EV, is the measure of work performed, expressed in terms of the budget authorized for that work. In other words, the value of the work actually completed so far, based on the budget. You calculate earned value by multiplying the budget for the project or BAC by the percent of actual work that's been completed up to the current date.

EV = BAC x actual % complete

Actual cost

Actual cost, or AC, is the total cost actually incurred up to a specific time. Calculate AC by summing up all labor and material costs, along with any other expenses, that have been incurred for the activity up to the current date.

EVM Steps

Once you've calculated the planned value, earned value, and actual cost for an activity, or for the entire project, you can determine exactly where things stand in relation to the cost baseline you set during planning. Any departure from the baseline is known as a variance.

Cost variance, or CV, is the difference between what a project has earned to date and what it has cost.

CV = EV – AC

If the CV is a negative number, it means the project or activity you're monitoring is over budget.

You can convert CV values into performance indicators that allow you to compare the current project against the indicators for other projects, or compare the performance of the same project at different stages. The cost performance index, or CPI, is determined by dividing EV by AC.

CPI = EV / AC

CPI > 1 = under budget.

CPI < 1 = over budget.

To express the cost performance as a percentage, multiply the CPI by 100.

Case Study: Question 3 of 4

Scenario

For your convenience, the case study is repeated with each question.

Your company, an energy provider, is working on a project to install wind turbines for a commercial customer. You're leading a team of 10 engineers, mechanics, and general construction employees. The project has an estimated completion date of six months and a budget of $23 million.

Answer the following questions in order.

Question

The turbine installation has finally started. You get an e-mail from one of the engineers, Dale, stating that you need to reduce the number of turbines from 15 to 12.

What are appropriate steps to take in response to the change request?

Options:

1. Find out if the change request to reduce the number of turbines was initiated by the client or someone else
2. After careful analysis, you decide that you will reduce the scope by two turbines, and make sure to document your decision by updating the scope baseline and project schedule
3. Conduct a detailed analysis to determine how reducing the number of turbines would impact the project's scope, budget, and other performance parameters
4. Agree with Dale that it makes sense from a financial perspective and implement the change to the plans without conducting a detailed analysis
5. Inform all stakeholders about the change request, whether or not you update the plans and project scope document

Answer

Option 1: This option is correct. The first thing you need to do when responding to a change request is determine who initiated the request and what type of change they've asked for. You also need to understand the factors that led to the request – like customer demands, changes in legislation, or technical difficulties.

Option 2: This option is correct. When faced with a change request, be sure to document your decision. Update the scope baseline, schedule or other project information as required.

Option 3: This option is correct. Before making a decision about making changes to the original plan for 15 turbines, you need to consider many factors, including the potential impact on scope, budget, and schedule.

Option 4: This option is incorrect. Without knowing who made the request and why, you shouldn't implement any changes, no matter if you agree with them or not.

Option 5: This option is incorrect. If you approved the change, you would need to inform stakeholders about it. However, there is no need to inform them if you end up rejecting the change request.

Case Study: Question 4 of 4

Scenario

For your convenience, the case study is repeated with each question.

Your company, an energy provider, is working on a project to install wind turbines for a commercial customer. You're leading a team of 10 engineers, mechanics, and general construction employees. The project has an estimated completion date of six months and a budget of $23 million.

Answer the following questions in order.

Question

The turbines have all been installed and the project is coming to a close. Overall the project was mostly successful, but it ended up taking eight months and costing just over $22 million.

What actions should you take to help close the project successfully?

Options:

1. Meet with your team to discuss lessons learned - in particular, the importance of researching environmental testing companies early because the one you contracted was short staffed, which caused delays
2. Store all the lessons learned and archived project information using your company's information management system so you can access it in the future
3. Meet with Dale to explain that reducing the number of turbines did save the client money, but that next time he needs to provide more detail in change requests
4. Since the customer hasn't communicated otherwise, tell your team that the project has been a success
5. Write a story to be posted on your company's internal website describing the project's success

Answer

Option 1: This option is correct. No matter how a project ends, a few project closure meetings may be appropriate. One thing you might discuss is lessons learned - what went well and should be repeated next time, and what didn't go well and how the next project can be improved.

Option 2: This option is correct. When you close a project, you need to perform administrative closure activities. One of these activities is to ensure all the necessary paperwork is completed and archived - for instance, customer or sponsor sign-offs and finalized project files.

Option 3: This option is correct. One of the project closure activities is to give feedback. You should do this not only if team-mates gained any new skills, certifications, or showed leadership capabilities, but also if they underperformed so they can improve.

Option 4: *This is an incorrect option. Part of conducting closure meetings is to gain the customer's acceptance and communicate whether or not there will be future interactions. No communication doesn't necessarily mean the customer is satisfied.*

Option 5: *This is an incorrect option. Although you probably want to share the good news of a successful project, this isn't one of the actions that will lead to successfully closing a project.*

LEAD YOUR PROJECT LIKE A PRO

There are three elements of a successful project result: a high-performing team, high-quality deliverables, and effective communication.

In this course I'll show you how to communicate the right information to the right stakeholders, and how to track your project's key data. You'll discover ways to uncover and satisfy stakeholders' needs within the project boundaries. And you'll find out how trust can be developed and an environment created where project work is completed to specification, on time and within budget. Let's begin.

Manage a Successful Project

1. Get the Communication Right
2. How to Track Your Project: Key Data
3. How Do You Keep Stakeholders Engaged?
4. Manage Conflict with Flair
5. Exercise: Be an Effective Project Lead

GET THE COMMUNICATION RIGHT

Let's say that you've been put in charge of a new project. You work for a "traditional" cookie company, and you've been asked to develop a range of gluten-free cookies.

In any project, communication is vital, and the project manager is the hub of communication. Project managers spend 90% of their time communicating, whether with external stakeholders, project team members, suppliers, or other managers within the organization. If your communication is not well thought out and delivered effectively, you're in danger of wasting a huge amount of time and money.

Communicating the right information to the right stakeholders using the right methods can be the difference that leads to project success, while miscommunication is a path to missed deadlines and defective deliverables. Sometimes privacy is also a factor; communicating sensitive information to the wrong stakeholder may cause a legal problem or an intellectual property leak.

Now let's take a closer look at how you can communicate effectively, and make it work for you and your project.

First, you need to have a communication management plan that identifies the who, what, why, when, and how of communication. Here's an example. Let's start with who – this covers the person who is responsible for communication, the person who authorizes it, and the groups and individuals who will receive the information.

Now, under the heading of what, we find the information to be distributed. This can include format, language, and level of detail. In most cases a list of reports and meeting plans will suffice. It might also be helpful to include the reason for distribution and any legal or regulatory constraints or why the communication is required.

[A communication management plan is displayed. Entries under the heading "What" include Issue Log, Change Log, Status Update, Progress Report, Project Forecast, Milestone Report, Invoice Report, and Contract Claims Report. Entries under the heading "Why" include Identify trends for EVP, For team leader review, and For COO review.]

The next heading – when – means the time frame and frequency of information distribution.

How covers the methods and technologies – for example, e-mail, text messages, conference calls, blogs, or press releases.

You'll also find it helpful to think about the three categories of communication methods: interactive communications, push communications, and pull communications.

Interactive communication is the most efficient way to ensure that all parties achieve a common understanding of what's being communicated. Use it when you need to make sure that the message is understood, or the sensitivity of the message requires that only the appropriate individuals are on the receiving end. Methods include face-to-face meetings, telephone calls, and video conferencing.

Push communication is when information needs to be distributed and timing is critical. The advantage is that it ensures the information is distributed; the disadvantage is it doesn't guarantee that the information is understood by all the recipients. Methods include status reports, milestone or deliverable reports, e-mails, and voice mails.

Pull communication is used when information needs to be distributed but isn't time sensitive and can be pulled in at the recipient's discretion. For example, all project documentation can be stored on a file server, secure web site or bulletin board for retrieval at any time.

So, how will you decide which communication method or technology to use? Well, here are some handy guidelines.

Where information is urgent, a pull communication method is not the most appropriate since pull methods are done on the receiver's schedule, and therefore the time frame may not be met.

When information needs to be distributed and timing is critical, push communication may be the appropriate.

When an immediate response is needed, and when information is sensitive or likely to be misinterpreted, interactive communication is the most appropriate. You will want to make sure that the person understands your message, and to be able to acknowledge it and address any clarifications or concerns they may have.

Bad news should always be given in an interactive manner: Face-to-face is the most open form of communication – since body language, facial expressions, and tone of voice may be understood – and will quickly show that the message was understood. If a face-to-face meeting is not possible, a web conference or a phone call is a better choice than an e-mail.

Good news is best given in person or by voice – you may wish to inform people that results of the taste tests have been positive – but following up in writing and sharing it with peers and superiors will help promote the goodwill of management for the project.

When stakeholders or team members are geographically dispersed, teleconferencing and video conferences may be used. For example, perhaps the proposed packaging for the new product range is a major departure from existing designs, and you want to see people's reaction to it.

Where information has to be transferred quickly to one or more persons, e-mail will probably be appropriate.

Overall, knowing when and how to communicate by applying these techniques outlined here will give you a big advantage in developing your project and bringing it to a successful outcome.

HOW TO TRACK YOUR PROJECT: KEY DATA

You are developing a range of gluten-free cookies for your company, a "traditional" cookie manufacturer. As the work progresses, you'll need to collect work performance data in order to gauge progress and to make sure that everything is OK. But what data should you collect, and how – and whom should you share it with?

First of all, I should explain that work performance data is raw data – status information. It reflects the current status of the various project parameters, such as scope, time, quality, and cost.

Basically, if the project manager doesn't know the amount of work that's been completed or the actual costs, then the project is at risk of being over budget and behind schedule. Knowledge is power.

This data enables you, the project manager, to compare what is occurring to what was planned, and to create meaningful status reports. It also guides you as to where actions may need to be taken because the project has in some way gone off track, when measured against planned baselines. For example, from evaluation of a missed milestone, the cause can be analyzed and a solution can be implemented before the overall due date is missed.

So, now we turn to what data you should be collecting. Here are some examples of work performance data. The categories are all related. For example, in terms of milestones, you need to ask whether the key targets are being met.

If there are too many defects, you will go over budget and take too much time; perhaps large number of trial cookie batches have been spoiled. In terms of actual costs, you need to look at the budget and ask how much has been spent to date, and how much is left.

The number of change requests may mean there is more work to do – for example, potential customers may think the range of cookie recipes is too narrow, so more resources will need to be allocated to address this. So, how should the data be gathered?

There are various ways. Data is compiled commonly via status meetings, project management software, accounting systems, and quality assurance databases.

So let's remind ourself why the data is useful. The performance data enables the project manager to monitor the project to compare what is actually happening to the planned baselines. By comparing against the plan you can recognize problems before a deliverable is missed or the team runs out of money.

Another example of using data is when we compare the percentage of work completed and the actual costs against the planned costs. Analyzing variances between planned and actuals can uncover whether or not the costs will continue, and therefore whether the project will complete within budget. Perhaps the cost variance was a single issue – for example, in the cookie research, a temporary shortage of some ingredient, leading to a price spike – and all other costs though will continue as planned. This is critical for forecasting final costs.

Performance information needs to be at an appropriate level for each audience. For example, senior management may be interested in high-level status information regarding the health of the project. Milestone status, major risk, and final forecasted budget are areas that paint a big picture of the project.

Conversely, the project team will be more concerned with details. For example, work to be completed in the next period, current status of risk and issues, and a summary of approved changes are more relevant to those who are actually doing the work.

The communication plan illustrates the possible information needs by incorporating the who, what, when and why of communications. This will help determine the distribution of work performance data.

Once you've grappled with the features of work performance data and learned how to use it to your benefit, you'll be in a much better position to bring about a successful outcome for your cookie project.

HOW DO YOU KEEP STAKEHOLDERS ENGAGED?

You are on your way to developing your new line of cookies. You need to keep all the stakeholders engaged.

Stakeholders are groups and individuals that can influence the project. The sponsor, the customer, end users, and outside organizations are some of the potential stakeholders. Stakeholder management involves creating and cultivating relationships for the benefit of the project. The goal is to discover and satisfy their needs within the project boundaries.

Stakeholders have various needs and levels of engagement. They should be identified as early as possible and documented on a spreadsheet or a stakeholder register. As new people are identified they can be added.

From the register of stakeholders, their level of engagement can be analyzed and documented. A separate engagement matrix may be useful. The current level of stakeholder engagement can be compared against the necessary level for project success.

There's a number of engagement classifications. "Unaware," fairly obviously, means that a stakeholder, or potential stakeholder, is unaware of the project's purpose. A "resistant" stakeholder is aware of the project's purpose but against change. A "neutral" stakeholder is aware of the project's purpose but neither for nor against it. A "supportive" stakeholder is aware of the project's purpose and in favor of a change. And a "leading" stakeholder is actively engaged in ensuring the project's success. These engagement levels should be added to the previously developed stakeholder register. These individuals are often identified as Change Agents.

And now that you're aware of where stakeholders stand in terms of your project, you can use your communication and interpersonal skills to engage them further, or to keep them engaged. Here are some guidelines that will help you.

First, be sure to articulate clearly and concisely.

Collaborate and cooperate in finding solutions where possible.

Distinguish stakeholders' needs from wants, and satisfy stakeholders' requirements without negatively impacting project objectives.

Build trust – communicate openly and honestly; follow through on commitments and don't make promises you can't keep.

Demonstrate active listening by providing verbal feedback and encouraging the speaker to continue. Ask questions and paraphrase what the speaker has said.

When stakeholders clearly understand project objectives, benefits, and risks, it is easier for them to be active supporters of the project – and therefore it's easier for the project to succeed.

For example, let's say that the company's production manager, Alan, is completely opposed to your project. He attends meetings grudgingly, and often doesn't reply to your e-mails. He feels that the trend toward gluten-free products is a fad, and that resources devoted to it will be wasted, that his department is too busy to handle it, and that it conflicts with the company's "traditional" image. What can you do or say to win him over?

In a face-to-face meeting, you could start by saying that you recognize and respect Alan's concerns, and then offer evidence that "gluten-free" is not just a fad, backed up by scientific and market research and statistics that you have compiled. You could point out that the company would miss out on a large potential market by failing to diversify, and might be left behind by its competitors.

Next, you could tell Alan that you respect his experience and expertise. You are asking for his ideas and insight.

You recognize that Alan needs to maintain production of his existing line, and wants to see continuity in everything the company does. Meanwhile, you need to make the new product line a reality, and you want to change the company's image to something more modern and cool.

You make a commitment to continue to compile further information as it becomes available. You agree to take any evidence to the contrary under consideration, and to remain open-minded as to whether the company should be involved in the gluten-free market in the medium to long term. You emphasize the idea of being part of the same team, with the company's best interests at heart.

You listen carefully to Alan's concerns; you are polite; you make notes; you offer to make some changes in the way you'll communicate with him from now on.

You know something? It's been a productive meeting. Your project is in a better place now.

MANAGE CONFLICT WITH FLAIR

Relationships within a team are a crucial element in the project's success. So, what will you do if conflict arises within the team?

High-performing teams manage conflict in an effort to develop trust, and to create an environment where project work is completed to specification, on time and within budget.

There are two types of conflict: functional and dysfunctional. Functional conflict is healthy and is simply a difference of opinion. Sometimes great ideas result from functional conflict.

Dysfunctional conflict, on the other hand, tears teams apart and may lead to delayed results, cost overruns, and product defects. Dysfunctional conflict should be addressed as soon as possible.

The good news is there are five techniques you can consider for addressing dysfunctional conflict.

The technique with the longest-lasting effect is collaboration. It involves identifying the root cause of the problem, and collaborating on the solution. Solving the cause of conflict so that all parties are satisfied is a win–win solution, and can build a stronger relationship. Use collaboration when there is enough time to have a difficult conversation.

The second technique is called smoothing. This means concentrating on the positive – whether that's the end goal or the wonderful skills that each party brings to the project. Smoothing is a short-term solution and can be a win–win initially. It's useful when the conflict is situational and the parties generally have a good relationship, or the stakes are not high.

Next, when agreement can't be reached by collaboration, then compromise may be the best choice. This is technically a lose-lose scenario, because all parties must give in on one or more desired outcomes. When compromises occur, both parties are likely to remember the previous result, and during the next interaction may be more stubborn and less likely to cooperate. This is generally a last resort.

Avoiding is when one or more parties refuse to even address the conflict. It can destroy the relationships just for the sake of winning. The only time avoiding is appropriate is when the conflict is really not worth wasting time on trying to resolve it.

The last approach is forcing – this is when one party demands action or output from the other without any collaboration. This is also a last resort, because it destroys relationships. The party that is being forced to act either will employ the avoidance tactic or will expect payback in the future.

Let's use an example from your cookie project to examine these approaches to conflict.

Let's suppose that Linda, who represents the accounting function on the team, has had a falling out with David, who manages the R&D group. David's already spent virtually his whole budget on trying out different types of gluten-free flour. Now he wants to try quinoa flour, which is super expensive.

You feel that the rift is due to a breakdown in communication. David wasn't clear about units of weight, which led Linda to believe that he was ordering much less flour than was actually the case. Then, to compound matters, she signed off on an invoice without checking it closely.

You meet with both of them at the same time and point out that there was never intention to mislead anyone. Nothing can be done about past mistakes now, but David and Linda can both commit to communicating more openly and clearly in the future, and to working more collaboratively for the good of the project. So, this solution is a combination of collaborating and smoothing.

A compromise might be if Linda agrees to advance David half the money he wants for the quinoa flour, and he agrees to work in smaller trial batches.

The approach of avoiding would not have had a good outcome here. It's essential that Linda and David maintain a functioning relationship if the necessary research is going to be conducted. A willingness to address any conflict is essential on both of their parts.

Finally, forcing would probably not have been a good outcome either. Linda could simply have refused to advance any more money, in which case either you would have had to go to the project sponsor and involve her in the problem – which wouldn't reflect well on your leadership abilities – or the range of trial recipes would have been narrower than you would have liked.

So, it looks like you've handled this outbreak of team conflict with a bit of flair. Good job!

EXERCISE: BE AN EFFECTIVE PROJECT LEAD

1. Exercise Overview

For a project to be successful, you need to know which data to track and how, and which mode of communication to use for specific purposes. Keeping stakeholders engaged and overcoming project conflicts are also key to an effective project.

In this exercise, you'll demonstrate that you can

- communicate project information appropriately
- identify key project data
- engage stakeholders appropriately, and
- manage a project conflict

2. Exercise: Be an Effective Project Lead

Case Study: Question 1 of 4

Scenario

For your convenience, the case study is repeated with each question.

Ralph is a senior localization project manager overseeing the translation of a cosmetics company's web site into multiple languages. He needs to make sure he tracks the right data, communicates appropriately, and handles any difficult conflicts.

Answer the questions in the given order to manage his project effectively.

Question

As the project manager, Ralph needs to send a status report to the marketing manager, a senior manager at the client company, with information about the progress of the web site translation.

What are appropriate questions that Ralph should ask himself in relation to high-level performance data to be included in the status report?

Options:

1. How much time on average does it take to translate one page of content?
2. What percentage of each language web site translation has been completed so far?
3. How much of the total budget has been spent on the review phase?
4. How much time has been spent on correcting translation errors?
5. What kind of corrections are the translation reviewers making?
6. Are we going to meet the milestone of 50% of total content translated by the end of the month?

Answer

Option 1: *This option is incorrect. Finding out the duration of small, specific project tasks is not an important consideration for the high-level status report. This kind of detail is more likely to concern the project team carrying out the translation work.*

Option 2: *This option is correct. Data about the percentage of work complete is vital in getting a clear idea of the project scope. In addition, it enables Ralph to find out if he's hitting his project milestones.*

Option 3: *This option is correct. Ralph's status report should include information about the actual costs. Without this information, he* won't know if his project is at risk of going over budget.

Option 4: This option is correct. Issues related to the quality of the translated content is a key factor to include in Ralph's status report. The quality of the output can also have a domino effect on his project's schedule and budget.

Option 5: This option is incorrect. This is an example of something that would involve the project team members, and does not concern senior management at the client company.

Option 6: This option is correct. Work performance data related to time, and specifically milestones, is a crucial piece of information for high-level status reports.

Case Study: Question 2 of 4

Scenario

For your convenience, the case study is repeated with each question.

Ralph is a senior localization project manager overseeing the translation of a cosmetics company's web site into multiple languages. He needs to make sure he tracks the right data, communicates appropriately, and handles any difficult conflicts.

Answer the questions in the given order to manage his project effectively.

Question

Case Study: Question 3 of 4

Scenario

For your convenience, the case study is repeated with each question.

Ralph is a senior localization project manager overseeing the translation of a cosmetics company's web site into multiple languages. He needs to make sure he tracks the right data, communicates appropriately, and handles any difficult conflicts.

Answer the questions in the given order to manage his project effectively.

Question

Access the learning aid Be an Effective Project Manager and read the conversation between Ralph and Sumie.

What principles for keeping stakeholders engaged does Ralph correctly apply?

Options:

1. He explains his points clearly to Sumie
2. He helps to build trust with Sumie by being honest and following through on his commitment
3. He distinguishes between his wants and needs and Sumie's
4. He paraphrases Sumie's concern and encourages her to speak
5. He explores a possible solution to Sumie's concern

Answer

Option 1: This option is correct. Ralph expresses his reasons for not wanting to hire a graphic design agency articulately and concisely.

Option 2: This option is correct. Ralph is open about his suggestion to find a graphic design agency and makes a realistic promise to hire a reasonably priced agency.

Option 3: This option is incorrect. Ralph focuses on his needs - getting the project finished on time - and as a result misinterprets Sumie's concerns.

Option 4: This option is incorrect. Ralph could have handled this conversation better if he had allowed Sumie to finish speaking. He also inaccurately paraphrases Sumie's issue, and didn't demonstrate effective listening skills.

Option 5: This option is correct. Ralph doesn't dictate his needs to Sumie and instead shows that he's willing to cooperate to discover a workable solution.

Case Study: Question 4 of 4

Scenario

For your convenience, the case study is repeated with each question.

Ralph is a senior localization project manager overseeing the translation of a cosmetics company's web site into multiple languages. He needs to make sure he tracks the right data, communicates appropriately, and handles any difficult conflicts.

Answer the questions in the given order to manage his project effectively.

Question

Access the learning aid Be an Effective Project Manager and read the conflict that has developed between Ralph and a senior translator, Michael.

What strategy should Ralph use in this project conflict situation?

Options:

1. Focus on the fact that the project's on schedule thanks to Michael's work and that the translation team may not even require a translation memory tool

2. Advise Michael that he will possibly look into using a translation memory tool later on in the project lifecycle if absolutely necessary

3. Tell Michael that while he appreciates his expert opinion, he is the project manager in charge and that his decision is final

Answer

Option 1: *This is the correct option. This is an example of a smoothing strategy that focuses on the positives to achieve a short-term win-win outcome. As Ralph and Michael have a good relationship, and the effect of translation tool on the project appears to be minimal, this is the most effective strategy.*

Option 2: *This option is incorrect. This is an avoiding strategy and*

should only be used as a last resort. It may also damage Michael and Ralph's relationship in the long term.

Option 3: *This option is incorrect. By forcing Michael to accept his decision, Ralph is at risk of destroying his relationship with Michael. Michael may also expect Ralph to agree to his demands in the future in exchange for accepting his decision on this occasion.*

Learning Aid

Be an Effective Project Manager

Purpose: *Use this learning aid to review a conversation between a project manager and a stakeholder, to learn about a conflict situation, and to answer two practice questions.*

Stakeholder dialog

During the project, one of the translation supervisors, Sumie, raises a concern about translating text embedded in images. Follow along as Ralph and Sumie have a conversation about it.

Sumie: I really don't think we should be working directly with the images. I'm not used to using image editing software. We're not graphic designers after all.

Ralph: What I'm picking up on is that you want to make sure that the images get translated as quickly as possible, and need some quick training, right? We're both in the same boat. Getting these images translated fast is one of my priorities too.

Sumie: That's not what I'm saying. My main concern is the quality of the finished images. Maybe we should...

Ralph: What, hire some contract graphic designers? It might be a good idea but I'm just worried that it'll add to our costs. Our budget is fairly limited as it is. It might also result in us pushing out our production schedule even further if the graphic designers can't provide a quick turnaround.

Sumie: Well, like I said, for me the most important thing is the quality of the finished images.

Ralph: OK, I'll tell you what. I'll contact some graphic design agencies for quotes. If I can find a reasonably priced agency who can commit to a one-day turnaround for the images, we'll hire them. And if you're happy with the quality of the images, we'll keep them for the rest of the project.

Conflict Situation

Michael is a senior translator who has worked with Ralph for over 10 years and has a positive relationship with him. However, at the start of the project, Michael has a disagreement with Ralph. Michael believes they should be using a translation memory tool. He argues that this will help translators do the work quicker as it can help reduce time spent doing repetitive translations. Ralph, however, thinks it's a minor issue. In his experience as a senior localization project manager, he believes it won't have any significant impact on the project duration, and that it's irrelevant anyway since the project is currently on schedule. They've had a number of meetings about the issue without a resolution. Michael has also rejected the idea of using a translation memory tool for just some of the web pages and wants it rolled out for the entire website.

www.ingramcontent.com/pod-product-compliance
Lightning Source LLC
Chambersburg PA
CBHW070114230526
45472CB00004B/1247